MYSTERIES
OF BRITAIN

MYSTERIES OF BRITAIN

First published in the UK in 2013

© Demand Media Limited 2013

www.demand-media.co.uk

Printed and bound in China

ISBN 978-1-909217-01-0

Contents

Introduction

As we all know too well, life if often full of surprises, some good, some bad and some unexpected. When we have time to think about our lives, our family and the places and surroundings in which we live, it can be surprising just how many

RIGHT Historical sign, Wareham

RIGHT Historical sign, Wareham

DORSET
ANY PERSON WILFULLY INJURING ANY PART OF THIS COUNTY BRIDGE WILL BE GUILTY OF FELONY AND UPON CONVICTION LIABLE TO BE TRANSPORTED FOR LIFE
BY THE COURT

unanswered, unsolved and unsearched stories actually surround us. There is, however, absolutely no reason why these anomalies or intriguing mysteries cannot be delved into, unraveled and solved.

The curiosity of ordinary people have been the backbone of many of the mysteries exposed here and without a doubt there are many, many more to be uncovered. Regardless of whether the root of an unsolved mystery be family related, architectural, or just something that is debated over and over again in your local area, there is absolutely no reason why any particular mystery cannot be solved.

The Little Book of Mysteries of Britain begins by uncovering an array of historical mysteries, exposing the tales of the past that are sitting right underneath us in the present. From the

ABOVE Stonehenge

secrets of 17th and 18th-century smuggler's tunnels to the flight of Mary, Queen of Scots, this is just a glimpse at the vast number of intriguing and often unresolved myths, mysteries and legends that are very often right under our noses in everyday life.

Fastidiously sorting out fact from fiction, each new mystery guides us through a fascinating process of discovering evidence that both proves and disproves historical theories and legends about different British mysteries.

Not only are particular mysteries researched, studied and explained in detail, each different example should

BELOW The Story of Kirdford

also teach you a variety of basic research skills so that if there is a local mystery in your life, and you fancy the challenge of getting to the bottom of it, you will feel confident about how to start getting your very own investigations underway. Proving also to be a good 'do-it-yourself' guide to uncovering 'Mysteries of Britain', it will hopefully give you some tricks of the trade, as well as the tools you need for the job, allowing you to navigate your way through archives, interpret archi-

tectural buildings and landscapes. You will be equipped and confident to take your own local historical mysteries by the horns and prove or disprove those local myths and legends, putting them into a historical context and settling any long-standing arguments for good.

The second part of the Little Book of Mysteries of Britain moves on to look at the geographical landscape that surrounds us, on a quest to unearth a variety of landscape mysteries that we perhaps just drive past and take for granted. They all, however, have a historical and fascinating story to tell. These landscapes did not just appear by magic; they are all saturated with the history of our great country.

From the fascinating revelations about the British landscape before the Ice Age to the ingenuity of the Tower People of Shetland, some quite remarkable aspects of the land we live on are revealed. The tour of the British Isles detailed

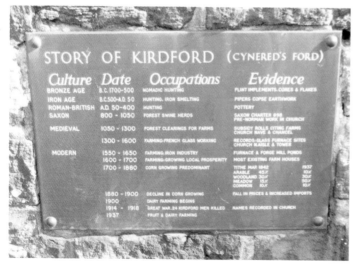

here highlights just how our landscape is laden with our past, and how it has influenced our present.

Our country's long history is hidden everywhere in the local present - in towns, villages, in the countryside, and on the landscape. With a little bit of knowledge, research and sometimes luck, the story behind that monument you pass every day, mysterious hidden passageway in your house, or chalk carving on the hill can be unlocked and discovered for the first time. We are often oblivious to how our long and magical history is all around us. This will hopefully open your eyes to just what can be discovered with a little curiosity and know-how.

Chapter 1

The Secrets of the Smugglers' Tunnels

FAR RIGHT The Ship Inn, Porthleven

In the 17th and 18th centuries Britain was awash with smuggling. It was rife in Kent, Northumberland, Wales and Scotland. In the southwest they say this was bigger business than farming.

Cornish smugglers were an inventive bunch and called themselves 'free traders' and were very proud of their ability to outsmart the revenue men who were employed to catch them. They hid their contraband in barrels with false bottoms and disguised tobacco as twists of rope. The smuggled goods were hidden in bedrooms, chapels, mansions, and cellars for hundreds of years.

In a Cornish fishing town, 12 miles east of Penzance, local legend has it that it was a hotbed for smuggling tea, brandy, and tobacco in the 17th and 18th centuries. Having advertised his Cornish pub, The Ship Inn in Porthleven, as a 'smuggling inn' for many years, the landlord is convinced that there has to be some element of truth in it just because of the sheer number of stories about the subject.

Was the pub directly linked to smuggling or not? Although there is no hard evidence, for 20 years the locals have been telling stories of smuggling, hidden passage ways, tunnels to the cliffs, and allegedly down in his cellar there is a covered up entrance to a tunnel.

In the 18th century, taxes and smuggling were at an all time high. A cup of tea would cost you six times in Britain as it would in France, and a glass of brandy five times more. No surprise then that people would take huge risks in bringing their duty free contraband ashore. But how did they actually do it? Are there actually tunnels in the landlord's cellar, or is that just a good Cornish yarn?

The first obvious difficulty to address is what evidence will have survived, when it was a practice that people were trying to hide so very well in the first place.

In the cellar, the first thing that needs to be established is what two blocked up shoots were used for. By making a plan of the cellar and a plan of the first floor, it can been seen how they line up. It draws a blank – the two shafts that the landlord highlighted in fact rise in the wrong place. The main one architecturally couldn't have been used as a back door for

RIGHT National Archives

LEFT A nearby smuggling hotspot: South West Coast Path Looking south west towards Kingsand and Cawsand, the latter to the left. Before 1844 Kingsand was in Devon and Cawsand in Cornwall. They are both now Cornish villages. In 1804 it was estimated that as many as fifty smuggling vessels operated from Cawsand Bay

contraband booze because it comes up in the middle of the building. Conclusion: the shafts have nothing to do with it!

Working out how the Ship Inn could have looked during the 18th century is also integral to the mystery. This can be done by focusing in on everything about the building and surroundings that date back to that time and earlier, meanwhile totally ignoring anything else that was built later. Windows often give a great clue to the smuggling era, especially wonky ones. Pre-Edwardian windows often didn't line up properly.

The National Archives can also be of great help in trying to find evidence of an official story. Is there documentary proof that smuggling did in fact take place in Porthleven? Look for official accounts and breakdowns for hard evidence – criminal records are a good starting point. In this instance a court case is found documented against a group of smugglers. They were tried for killing a customs officer who was whipped to death on his way to intercept the smugglers. It is discovered that smuggling in Porthleven was in fact pretty big business. But so far nothing has linked it to the Ship Inn.

So many boats and such a large, open coastline was an invitation for smugglers to bring contraband in. In addition to that, the Cornish were very poor people, they therefore needed the smuggling to boost their income. Everybody did it from the poor to the rich. If a smuggler was caught and he'd gone to court, he often got away with it, because the judge was probably buying the goods from him as well! A somewhat corrupt society, but apparently, a lovely one!

The most likely place that was linked to smuggling was a cave just along the coast from the village and it is thought that it linked up with a large house called Methleigh Manor.

Records at The National Archives also reveals that the landlords of the Ship Inn had lived at Methleigh Manor, putting the pub right back in the middle of everything. The wealthy land owning family were trying to get one of their men put into the customs house, so that they had an insider on the job.

Although the concept of smugglers tunnels in the pub were not correct and at Methleigh Manor, it is thought that tunnels exist along the coastline near the manor house, and that on the coastal path on the cliff tops the entrance to the tunnel could be located.

Two square openings side by side in the rocks in a cove in fact mark the (what is assumed) manmade entrance to a cave; because of the shape there is not much chance that the sea has done that naturally as they are both the same height and dimensions. If the manor house is on top of the hill above the cove then this may have uncovered smuggling central.

Evidence at The National Archives also directly links the owners of the manor house and the Ship Inn with smuggling. The actual customs book that the officers wrote in when they were recording the smuggling incidents proves this. There is a letter from the owner himself, asking permission to move goods up and down the coast, which had allegedly washed up on the shore! The wealthy family had rights of salvage and the letter relates to his request to the 'right of wreck' that just so happens to start from the coastline from the Ship Inn. The evidence proves that they were definitely involved in smuggling, or at the very least had the opportunity to be so.

On further investigation of the coves, however, it is found that the

LEFT A Smugglers Tunnel

Smugglers

London, Published June 1 1816, by W Miller &c. Albemarle Street, and J. Walker & Greasy Street, Berry Square

cave openings are in fact natural and not manmade after all. Over thousands of years a watercourse has eaten its way right through the cliff face. That doesn't mean, however, that it wasn't used by smugglers and for storage of their goods. The smugglers didn't necessarily need any tunnels; they just needed a safe place on the coast to be able to drop the contraband.

The evidence against the Methleigh Manor family is circumstantial yet pretty damning, and certainly seems to stack up against them. It is thought that they were certainly involved in the smuggling operation at the very least. Hard history comes from the documents and paper trail. The family seemed to be the masters of the trade in the area, as well the owners of The Ship Inn.

The conclusion for the landlord of the Ship Inn: his 17th-century pub isn't! It is 18th century, described as newly built in the 1780s. The cellar tunnels aren't smugglers ones, and in fact there is no evidence of tunnels anywhere in the area! The link with the family from Methleigh Manor at the time is the only apparent smuggling connection.

FAR LEFT An illustration showing smugglers unloading contraband

LEFT Example of barrels used for smuggling

Chapter 2

Hidden Highwaymen

In Wiltshire, home to those mysterious white horses carved into the landscape and the puzzling ancient monument, Stonehenge, this mystery focuses on a small stone set on the side of a road, which marks the site of a 19th-century highway robbery.

In Devizes in Wiltshire, a local historian who has a passionate interest in the history of crime and punishment, is particularly intrigued by a highway robbery that took place in 1839, and one that has left as its legacy a curious and unexplained memorial. Seeing as she drives past the stone nearly every day located on the road between Devizes and Salisbury, she wants to find out about the inscription on the stone. It talks about four highwaymen that attacked and robbed a man from Imber. What was so important about this particular highwaymen's attack that made the locals pay for the stone?

At the beginning of the Victorian era attitudes to crime and punishment were changing and becoming more enlightened, and the local press was becoming more powerful. The geographical area is also interesting - on the edge of Salisbury Plain, which was a very dangerous place during the 18th century. On the periphery of a very poor rural area, crime was notoriously high. As there wasn't a police force, if you wanted anyone caught and punished, you had to do it yourself.

Life in the nearest town of Devizes in the 1830s would have been busy with merchants showing off their goods in the market square. It was where the banks and inns were built, and where money was exchanged. The Kennet and Avon canal that runs through the town would have brought trade to the town, as well as the Bath stone, from which many of the buildings were built. At the time the highwaymen were operating, Devizes would have been a very wealthy place – a town of rich merchants with rich pickings for robbers.

Gallows Ditch, the hanging green where convicted criminals met their end, is perfect proof of such brutal times of the past. By the end of the 18th century, the Dick Turpin model (where a chivalrous robber would take from the rich and give to the poor) had come to an end. In the early 19th century there would have been more desperate people who needed money just to feed their families. It was a time when people were no longer farmers on their own land, and if they lost their jobs there was no one to help, and they starved. Quite a lot of people who took to highway robbery were desperate.

1839 was in the middle of what

ABOVE On Walbury Hill, a typical Salisbury Plain landscape

became known as the Hungry Forties, a period of great depression especially in Wiltshire where local industry was dying. The Corn Laws of 1815 and 1828 had hiked up the price of bread, so for many the only way to survive

in the chase.

The man robbed by the four highwaymen on the stone was a Mr Matthew Dean who was returning from Devizes Fair, laden with cash, to his home in the village of Imber.

By searching the archives in London the intention is to find any information about the named robbers (Colclough, Saunders, Waters and Harris), their trial and punishment and also anything about their victim, Mr Dean. It is discovered that three of them had broken the law before.

On the stone itself is the following inscription: 'At this spot Mr Dean of Imber was attacked and robbed by four highwaymen in the evening of October 21st 1839 …'. As well as listing the names of the robbers, the stone has another message – 'this monument is erected by Public Subscription but as a warning to those who presumptuously think to escape the punishment God has threatened against Thieves and Robbers.' It was erected as a warning rather than as a monument.

The crime scene would have been a lonely place in 1839; at the top of a long hill the robbers chose their spot well. Although their victim was on

was to turn to a life of crime, regardless of the possible consequences. With no police force in action, the only way to stop a crime and catch the criminal was to 'raise a hue and cry'. Anyone who heard it was bound by law to join

horseback, the climb would have been tiring, therefore leaving him very vulnerable as he entered their trap.

The robbers, having stolen three £20 notes from Mr Dean, were caught after a three-hour 'hue and cry'. Colclough literally dropped dead in the middle of Salisbury Plain; the local press said that he was literally 'runned to death'.

The other three were caught and taken off to the magistrates. Sentence for robbery in Victorian times was severe, but were they just chancers or was it a well-planned crime?

The Grecian-style Courthouse in Devizes is an impressive building and where the robbers were presumably tried and sentenced as it was built in 1835, four years before the offence took place. Although the gallows were still in use, by the time of the robbery, model prisons had also been built and there was one in Devizes. The three surviving highwaymen were held there for six months at Her Majesty Queen Victoria's pleasure after being sen-

FAR LEFT Towpath Devizes. The towpath below the bridge over the Kennet and Avon Canal (Caen Hill Locks)

BELOW Devizes Courthouse built in 1835. Now fenced off and boarded up. Will it be found a role in the future. It is a listed building and is at risk

BELOW Port Arthur Prison Settlement Site

tenced 'to transportation to Australia for 15 years hard labour' as stated on the stone.

After they were transported, further investigation is discovered that reveals that they were shipped to Tasmania in 1940 on a ship called The Lord Lyndoch, and that Harris married another convict he met on board the ship. Details of their lives found in the convict archives indicate that their lives were pretty grim. Harris apparently tried to hang himself.

It is also discovered that the original stone has a twin, which was erected at the spot where Colclough dropped down dead (also in the middle of Salisbury Plain). Almost identical, except this one is much bigger and it tells the story of the robber Colclough who was buried without funeral rites at Chitterne.

A living relative of the victim, Matthew Dean's great, great grand-daughter, who still has a picture of him is also still alive. It turns out that he was quite a wealthy man and lived in Imber (which is now slap bang in the middle of a firing range on Salisbury Plain) in a big family house, half of which still stands. It was the family home for five generations. Although the date still showing on

ABOVE This painting dipicts a highway robbery

the outside of the house states incorrectly 1880, there is evidence of parts of it dating back to the late 17th or 18th century.

But why were the two stones put up at all? One theory is that it was the way local society banded together against criminal individuals. Farmers and landowners would have got together to put them up as a vested interest in protecting their livelihoods as a message to vagabonds and highwaymen, and also the labouring classes. Farmers therefore created action groups and clubs as a deterrent. Although this particular robbery is highlighted, evidence shows that there was an awful lot of this type of criminal activity at the time.

City Under the Sea

Dunwich, on the east coast of England was in the 13th century a huge bustling town with a population of nearly five thousand people, in fact half the size of London's. Then came two storms that changed its fate forever and wiped out nearly a quarter of the entire city. The sea has literally swallowed up Dunwich over the past 700 years.

Once the Saxon capital of East Anglia, Dunwich was the site of a thriving port by the 12th century and was one of the busiest places on England's east coast. It boasted 13 churches, about 1,600 houses, a massive city hall and five market squares. It was an extremely wealthy and powerful city with ship building yards catering for the richest customers in the country, including the King himself. The trade included both merchant and fishing; this extremely sprawling prosperous city would have been the place where most of the country's trade passed through. The importance of Dunwich to the national economy at the time, let alone the local area, cannot be over-stated.

Dunwich became of major importance during Norman times when it was a deep-water port, and therefore a trading centre as well as an ecclesiastical centre; it was an extremely rich town. The city was devastatingly

ABOVE Gateway ruins, Greyfriars, Dunwich

up, which inevitably sealed its fate. Without a port to trade from people gradually moved away and the city fell into ruin.

Although some vigorous research and writing about the men of the city has been carried out, there are still parts of the story unwritten and missing gaps to fill. In particular, the history of the geography of the area, which, bearing in mind that there is very little left of the original city, is a challenge in itself. In fact, creating an accurate bird's eye view of the lost city is something that until recently has never been done before.

With origins dating back to the early Bronze Age, Dunwich was the main trading port and sprawling metropolis. It's very hard to believe that such a big, bustling and indus-trious place could simply be wiped out leaving it now lying beneath the waves.

By looking at the stones and rocks on the beach for any evidence, although the vast majority of the medieval port has been washed away, with a little digging and some patience the shoreline still hides the sort of evi-dence that very much helps.

ripped apart by two hurricane storms and now all that remains is a ruined city. In 1286 the first storm virtually destroyed the harbour entrance, which naturally affected the livelihoods of everyone. Then in 1328 another worse storm hit, many lost their lives and the harbour was totally blocked

The local museum also houses a model that outlines the shape of the old city. The plans to create it came from medieval maps published in a 200-year-old book, although as a word of caution, these are renowned for not being particularly accurate.

The National Archives also holds calendars, which are printed transcripts of old documents. A transcript of an inquisition by Crown officials to find out what happened to Dunwich at the time of the storm, gives amazing incite into the damage and havoc that was caused when the storm hit.

The only landmarks that have survived are the ruins of the Franciscan Friary perched very close to where the present coastline has advanced. There are also the remains of a leper hospital situated at the furthest westerly point of the old city. It's the only part to have survived quite well, mainly due to the fact that it would have been located just outside the city wall. It is estimated that there is three times the size

of the existing village that stretches out to sea.

The church that was built on the leper hospital site long after the storms shows further useful information on its noticeboard. It shows how much of the original church there was in 1903 and how much had been further eaten by the sea by 1919 – most of it in fact, leaving just one buttress – the last existing buttress of the last medieval Dunwich All Saints

BELOW Remains of St James's Chapel, Dunwich, Suffolk

REMAINS OF ST. JAMES'S
CHAPEL DUNWICH, SUFFOLK

TO SIR CHARLES BLOIS BAR^T

COCKFIELD HALL YOXFORD

Church. The church was originally 44 metres long and very substantial. There is also further photographic evidence that documents how the church looked as a whole, and then how it gradually fell into the sea over the years.

By looking at a surviving medieval church, a good feel for the architecture that captures the time of Dunwich's heyday can be found. The round and square bell tower dominates the church, and the bells would have rung across medieval Dunwich calling its people to prayer. Legend has it that you can still hear the bells of Dunwich tolling under the sea.

Mapping the original medieval town is not so easy, even though local marine archaeologists have dived the historic site hundreds of times over the years, from which many surviving artefacts have been recovered. In view of this fact, however, it is the marine archaeologists who could possibly help again with this historical challenge.

With the aid of the assumedly inaccurate medieval map, a trip out sea in a boat equipped with an echo sounder and GPS navigation means that an attempt to start plotting the location of where each church was can be carried out. After all, they were the biggest structures and therefore more easily identifiable than anything else. Also, the large stone blocks that the churches were made from would have survived much better than any timber framed house that had been swamped by the sea. The information from the boat can then be translated into a sketch of the area. All of the churches in fact can be identified and then successfully mapped, so that for the first time a bird's eye view of medieval Dunwich can be created.

Information concerning the merchants of Dunwich is also uncovered which leads to conclusions with regard to the ultimate fate that sealed

RIGHT Dunwich All Saints Church Ruins 1904

LEFT Remains of Mediaeval Leper Hospital, Dunwich The present St James Church was built in the grounds of the former leper hospital

their city's doom. Some Latin scripts from the 14th century document what was happening in 1286. It appears that after the great storm a lot of land was washed into the sea and many houses were destroyed. The people of Dunwich worked for six years to try and repair the damage, i.e. unblock the ports. In the seventh year, however, the men of Southwold undid all this work by blocking the port up. With their neighbours turning on them because of trade competition, Dunwich didn't stand a chance and quickly turned into a ghost town, totally ruined.

Chapter 4

The Town of Black Silk

In the south east of England in Halstead, Essex, for over 150 years silk weaving was the main industry of the town, and women and children as young as eight years old worked in the local mills. A resident of the town wants to discover if one of her ancestors was in fact one of those children slaving away all hours god sends, working by candlelight. She worked in the Courtauld silk factory herself in the 1950s and her family have lived in the town for generations. The challenge is to unearth her family history, capture a snapshot of life in the Victorian silk industry, and figure out the link between the two.

The investigation starts by identifying the traces of Victorian Halstead. What buildings remain despite its 20th-century makeover, for example? What were the conditions like in the 19th-century silk industry? How long was the working day? How were the employees treated?

At the local archives the particular family tree in question can be studied in order to find out which members of the family actually worked at the silk factory.

The owner of the factory at the time, Samuel Courtauld, put many date stones on buildings around the town carved into blocks of red sandstone. 'SC' is on many of the stones and refers to the man himself, which

LEFT Courtauld Mill, Halstead

clearly indicates that not only was he an employer but also built many of the town's buildings. The Courtauld family evidently played a massive part in creating the town and supporting its inhabitants by providing a lot of work. They were, however, renowned as being tough employers.

Bought in 1825, they first bought the old corn mill to start the silk weaving factory. Townsford Mill was built in the 18th century, and when entrepreneur Samuel Courtauld bought it he replaced the water-powered mill wheels with cutting edge steam technology. The building at

first housed the spinning and weaving of yarn for his growing silk empire. The business flourished and they were renowned for making the black crepe famously widely worn during Queen Victoria's reign, following the death of her husband Prince Albert.

Courtauld quickly outgrew the mill and was forced to build a new factory just to weave the fabric, and in its heyday over 1,200 people worked in the factory.

The silk factory was demolished in the 1980s to make way for a supermarket, and the old mill itself is now an antiques centre. The remaining architecture inside highlights the very clever use of timber frame and many, many windows to let as much light into the building for the workers as possible.

By meeting people who are skilled in the original techniques of weaving helps greatly to find out more about what the workers would have been doing. There are three principles of weaving: shedding (throw the shuttle through), picking, and then beating. The silk looms were mechanical and they had 1,500 looms at one time in the weaving shed at Halstead.

When silk weaving began it was a cottage industry, but in the early 1800s factories sprung up with groups of weavers all working under the same roof. The invention of steam-driven looms transformed the industry as the increased speed of weaving meant larger profits. The Halstead factory was one of the first to implement steam looms, and by the middle of the 19th century the Courtauld workforce had grown to 600.

In the early 19th century silk workers in London had their wages fixed by magistrates. For bosses the rate was too high and for workers it was too low. Many of these London workers therefore moved to the Courtauld factory in Halstead. That didn't mean that the work conditions and their treatment were any better, however. Working six days a week on 12-hour shifts was the standard terms of employment, even for children as young as eight. Humiliation and even beatings were not uncommon for shoddy work or any sign of rebellion amongst the workers. It was certainly extreme and harsh working conditions for all.

Between 1833 and 1850 saw the passing of four Factory Acts with the aim of shortening the working week, as well as increasing educational

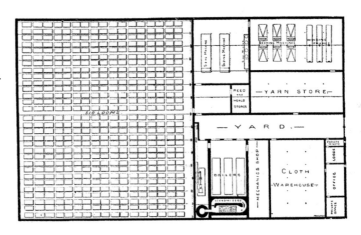

FAR LEFT Queen Victoria in black mourning silk

ABOVE Plan of a Weaving Shed

opportunities for the children who worked in the factories; naturally these were not so easy to enforce.

Silk weaving went into decline, however, in the middle of the 20th century and production at Halstead stopped in 1983; they were unable to

compete with the cost of silks woven in China and the Middle East.

Tracking down local people who have impressive collections of memorabilia including press cuttings and photographs, in this instance all about the Courtauld family, the factory and the people who worked there, is also integral to these types of investigation. In addition to such evidence, finding out just how much influence the Courtauld family had on the town as a whole is also key. A memorial celebrating the Golden Jubilee of Queen Victoria's reign presented to the town by George Courtauld in 1887 is a good example of such. There is even still a member of the family living in the town, another George, who is a direct descendant of the founder of the silk factory who even worked there himself before its closure.

In fact, it was family policy for them to actually work in the factory on the looms. Although this would now been seen as the management of a company setting a great example to it employees, in those days it was in fact taken for granted. By interviewing the surviving family member, George definitely gives the impression that

his ancestors did have the interests of their employees at heart and that it was a very close-knit community. One of George's great uncles had said that he hoped on his gravestone would be inscribed with 'he built good cottages'!

On the subject of cottages, the old factory cottages in the town are certainly surviving examples of how life used to be. The Victorians used to

ABOVE Example of Factory Cottages

FAR LEFT Children working in a mill in Macon, Georgia

love white bricks because it looked like stone, which meant that they could afford to dress their buildings. The windows are also eye catching due to the fact that in the 18th century panes of glass were quite small, then the Victorians pioneered a way of making glass panels much bigger. Big sash windows were in place by the 1840s, but the large panes of glass required for such a style were very expensive. The factory cottages show very pretty windows but with smaller individual panes set in an ornate frame, making them cheaper to produce. Factory Terrace cottages were built by Samuel Courtauld for his workers in 1872.

With an architectural study and search of the town, combined with the aid of old photographs, it is possible to create a visual image of what the factory and its immediate surrounding area would have looked like at the heart of industrial Halstead.

At the local archives family information can be researched, and in this particular instance it is with regard to the grandmother Annie Brooks and her great-grandmother, Sarah Ann Spurgeon. It seems they were both definitely silk weavers according to the 1881 census. According to the factory employment records, the great-grandmother started off in the factory as a winder in January 1876 at the age of 13. In 1880 she then moved to the power looms. The records state that she was a weaver, but she left in January 1895 to have a family and then reapplied for more work.

Some surprising facts about her great-great-grandmother also come

to light. She was not in fact a weaver but a charwoman and her great-great-grandfather, George Spurgeon died in 1867 at the age of 22, which would have put the family in a difficult position. A whole new line to the family tree comes to light as it is discovered that her great-great-grandmother later remarried and had more children.

BELOW Example of a Power Loom

Chapter 5

The Tower, The Queen and the Outlaws

In the Cheviot Hills just north of the border between England and Scotland was once Britain's frontier territory. This was a place where families seriously feuded for 300 years. A now-ruined Pele tower was at the centre of it all and it is thought that Mary Queen of Scots stayed there during a desperate flight to a lover in 1566. The question is did she really?

The area either side of the English and Scottish border is stark and barren, albeit beautiful. Home to bands of marauding extended families known as Border Reivers in the 15th and 16th centuries, many of them lived in little castles called Pele towers. There are hundreds of these dotted along the border.

A local farming couple have been intrigued by the mystery for many years and want to find out if the legend, which is still re-enacted annually, that Mary Queen of Scots actually stayed in the Pele tower in the middle of their cow field, is indeed fact or fiction. And what did that specific tower originally look like?

Mary was Queen of Scotland and a Catholic, and her right to the English throne occupied by her Protestant cousin, Elizabeth I, was disputed throughout her lifetime. The fourth Earl of Bothwell was her lover, and he was also appointed the job by the Scottish Government of policing

the lawless area in question. He was, however, reportedly as corrupt as the Reivers themselves!

The first place to start is with a map to establish where Queen Mary lived, in Jedburgh, and mark the route to Hermitage Castle, which was her destination. Even having to negotiate the rough terrain and landscape on horseback, although she would have definitely ridden by the tower, the question already arises, why would she have stopped off at this particular spot, when it would have only been an hour or so into the journey?

In order to be able to prepare a

useful visual image of what the tower would have originally looked like, detailed architectural investigations also have to commence. The tower looks like it was erected very quickly as the remaining stones look like they were just thrown together. This is most likely because a family would only have had the first summer of arriving there to get it up before the winter hit. The space inside the ruin would not have been very big at all.

Meeting with local historians is always the best way to add 'meat' to preliminary findings. In this particular case, they are used to find out as much as possible about Mary's ride past Fulton. In the 19th century a watch was found that Mary lost on her way to Hermitage, and it was found in a bog. A notorious Reiver called Little Jock Elliot of the Park had injured Mary's lover (the Earl of Bothwell) quite badly and she was travelling to his aid. How did a Reiver get away with such an act on an official? According to the local historian, this is where the large Reiver families become involved in the bigger picture. Names including the Grahams, the Armstrongs, the Bells, the Nixons, and the Elliots were all renowned for protecting and backing each other up if, even the most humble of border farmers, were under threat; the local mafia nonetheless! These families were also known for running huge extortion rackets, particularly the Grahams and the Armstrongs; they were really like modern day gangsters.

In terms of armour and protection they would have worn steel bonnets complete with earflaps and most would also carry a dagger. Even the clergy carried daggers because these border Reiver families were not adverse to even taking their quarrels to church with them!

The family living in Fulton Tower at the time of Mary's reported ride were the Turnball family, and it is discovered that they were supporters of

FAR LEFT Mary Queen of Scots

BELOW LEFT Clan Elliot Crest Badge

BELOW RIGHT Remains of Fulton Tower

THE TOWER, THE QUEEN AND THE OUTLAWS

BELOW Gilnockie
Tower

Mary, although no hard evidence has been found to definitely confirm that she stopped at the tower on her way to Hermitage. If she did, however, she would have been most welcome.

The Gilnockie Tower was the Armstrong's family seat and, in view of the fact that it has been restored, it provides excellent detailed information with regard to the precise architecture of the ruined Pele Tower at Fulton. Armed with more information

ABOVE Border reivers at Gilnockie Tower, from an original drawing by G. Cattermole

it is now possible to begin a hopefully accurate reconstruction of Fulton Tower. With closer examination, however, it is also thought that the Pele Tower remains are not the only building ruins on the site.

Whilst evidence of the criminal activity in the area at the time is also discovered, there is nothing yet found relating to Queen Mary's visit. One reason for this is that the area was like the Wild West, and it would have been very difficult for people to write down and document events accurately, when actually their main concern in life was not losing their heads.

Information about the Elliot family who lived in Redheugh also comes to light, and they appear to be one of the most notorious families in the area. The following extract about the family is documented: ' … the second family of Liddesdale, less numerous than the Armstrongs with whom they

BELOW Cheviot Hills

are frequently allied. They were as predatory as any clan on the frontier' and 'occasionally under English protection they received a subsidy from Queen Elizabeth against the Scots'. This shows that some of these families were actively trying to suppress the Scots.

A draft Act of Parliament from 1535 requiring property over a certain value to be fortified and include an external animal enclosure called a 'barmkin' is also uncovered. This information backs up the theory that there was another building in the vicinity of Fulton Tower.

Documentary evidence about the legendary Queen Mary ride seems to be elusive, however. Of course there remains much speculation in view of the fact that numerous secondary sources such as poems, songs and stories have been told about the mystery over the centuries. It is of course because of such (often verbal) traditions that keeps such myths alive for so many years.

The major and conclusive piece of primary evidence discovered is that the occupants of the tower in question were in fact allies of

ABOVE Example of a Pele Tower

Queen Mary and there is official correspondence that proves Mary did in fact make the ride. It also documents the precise date, that being the 15th October 1566. It is also confirmed that she did in fact make the journey so that she could be at the side of her wounded lover, Bothwell.

Chapter 6

Puzzle at the Palace

In Gwynedd in North Wales over-looking the Menai Straits, close to the city of Bangor and the Isle of Anglesey, there is a mystery that needs investigating. It is the mystery of a chicken farm that in fact began its life as a 13th-century legendary palace. Or did it? The Gibson family who have initiated the investigation bought the magnificent house, called Pen y Bryn, some 20 years ago.

The family want to find out if their suspicions are correct, and that their house was once much more than a chicken farm, but instead the 13th-century palace of Prince Llywelyn, the last Welsh born Prince of Wales. If enough evidence can be found to back up their

theory, it could turn their house into a Welsh national monument. Having searched the archives for nearly 20 years, the family still haven't found any conclusive evidence. In particular, they would like to know what the house looked like when the last Prince of Wales lived there in the 13th century. First, however, it has to be proved that the house was, in fact, definitely Llywelyn's palace.

The first port of call is to look at the geographical area and landscape, Roman and Bronze Age remains, and map it out so they have an idea of how the area looked in the 13th century. The position of the house is also key to this part of their investigation and will say a lot about whether it would have been a likely site for a Prince's palace. The landscape is certainly ancient, but there are layers and layers of different ages to dissect in order to identify how it would have been during the medieval period.

At The National Archives in London, it is hoped that letters can be found that Llywelyn wrote just before he died, from a place called Garth Kellin.

PUZZLE AT THE PALACE

BELOW The National Archives London

Is this really the palace Pen y Bryn, as some think it is, or was this the name of the Prince's house that was located somewhere nearby? Unfortunately, not much is found in London, so the next target is the archives in Wales.

Early in the investigation evidence is discovered that puts the house at the centre of a fair amount of controversy. Local newspaper archives reveal that they are by no means the first people to investigate the issue and most of the reports firmly suggest that the house was not Llywelyn's palace. It transpires that most of the local archaeologists think that the Prince's house was in fact

BELOW The National Archives London

built next to a Norman motte lying 300 yards east of Pen y Bryn.

Laid out typically like a Norman settlement, with the motte positioned for defence and the settlement below (called the bailey), Gwynedd Archaeological Trust looked at the site 10 years before to ascertain whether medieval life could have been centred there during Llywelyn's reign. In the bailey they found a big 'H'-shaped memorial hall and lots of pottery, which all suggests that this in fact was the centre of power.

It is generally agreed locally, and particularly by Cadw (who look after the built heritage of Wales) that Llywelyn's palace was at the motte and not Pen y Bryn. It transpires that they think a gentleman called William Thomas decided to build himself a brand new house close to the assumed Llywelyn site, but it had to look as fashionable as possible. He therefore most likely copied designs from other houses in the area. It is also thought that this house was built after the medieval period and that it is therefore not a medieval building at all. They in fact claim to have found the medieval building remains at the motte. Pen y Bryn therefore can't possibly be the Prince of Wales' original dwelling.

The site of Llywelyn's palace would have been the site of the most important dynasty in Welsh history. Llywelyn united the parts of Wales that were not under English rule and turned a country that was a patchwork of rival lordships into a single state and a powerful nation. Llywelyn became the first

prince of a united Wales, and also a very real threat to King Edward I. In 1282, on the brink of international power, Llywelyn died in mysterious circumstances and Wales was left to become part of the English empire.

The actual palace that is being searched for played a key role in the war between these two tough leaders, Edward I of England and Llywelyn the Last of Wales. By 1282 the mountains behind Pen y Bryn were swarming with English soldiers as Edward I surrounded the Welsh with a large army, with the intention of crushing Welsh independence. He offered Llywelyn a deal first, however, of £1,000 per year and an estate in exchange for Wales. Unsurprisingly Llywelyn rejected the offer and a month later he was dead, a supposed accident, leaving Wales in the hands of the English.

Before the English took

over, Wales was made up of small, undefended palaces that were protected from intruders by the natural mountainous landscape. This all changed forever once the English took control and they built many huge castles as a symbol of power; there was no mistaking who was then in charge.

Despite all of the research that has been done to date, if any new and hard evidence can be uncovered for the first time with regard to Pen y Bryn, it could rewrite the history books.

Looking closely at the outside of Pen y Bryn there is a small round-arched window that looks older than all the other Elizabethan windows. Inside the house it can be concluded that the constituent parts of the walls are either Elizabethan or Jacobean. Seeing as most old houses have been added to over the years, the cellar is a good place to start if looking

FAR LEFT King Edward I and his wife Eleanor of Castille

LEFT Statue of Llywelyn the Last

PUZZLE AT THE PALACE

RIGHT Caernarfon Castle, one of the most imposing of Edward's Welsh castles

BELOW Gwynedd

for the very earliest parts of a house.

The Pen y Bryn cellar is much smaller than the lounge above, the first oddity if they were the same age. Seeing as many medieval builders used a 16-foot measurement called a 'pole', they typically built in standard units – two, four, eight etc. The measurements of Pen y Bryn cellar and tower conform to this early system, but the house above doesn't. By measuring the whole house the measurements can then be translated to a scaled plan drawing. It looks like the cellar and the house's tower are the earliest parts of the building and were there before 1600, whilst the main house in the centre was built later on but directly on top. So, Pen y Bryn is built on a medieval site, although date wise this could mean anything from the Romans to the Tudors.

At the Bangor archives an 1846 map is found that shows Pen y Bryn quite clearly, and it also ties the house in with the manor of Aber. From a document dating back to 1284 it lists all the details of the Aber district at that time. It lists the land of the manor of Aber and says that a long house was at the centre of the manor. The long house described in the 1284 document is in fact Pen y Bryn and was also called Garth Kellin – three names for one house!

Of course the Norman motte still plays a huge part in proceedings and the conclusion is that Llywelyn probably had his court at the motte and his home and palace at Pen y Bryn.

Chapter 7

The Post Mistress who was a Spy

In the market town of Highworth in Wiltshire, a local James Bond-like character from the Second World War has long caused much intrigue and debate for the town's people. Was this person really the silver-haired postmistress who worked in the village? Her surviving grandson would like to find out exactly what she did during the war.

At the beginning of the Second World War, invasion of Britain by Hitler was a very real possibility. In 1940 Winston Churchill went about setting up a secret force embedded in the small country towns and villages of England. Ordinary people were at the very core of this resistance movement and were trained in guerrilla warfare. Vicars, shopkeepers and factory workers made up this web of undercover agents and they were called the Auxiliary Units. The mystery and mission - should one choose to accept it - is to find out if the local postmistress was really part of this top-secret operation and to what extent she was involved in it. She was also supposed to have been on Hitler's death list. Is this rumour or truth?

The lady in question was called Mabel Stranks. According to her grandson Brenan, since the death of Mabel in 1971, theories and rumours have circulated, claiming that she was more of a spy mistress than a postmis-

tress. Having signed up to the Official Secrets Act being a postmistress anyway, nothing else is known for sure about her possible 'other' activities.

The reason behind the speculation of Mabel's involvement with the Auxiliary Unit stems from one of her known roles as postmistress. It was her job to send new recruits arriving for training to the secret headquarters at nearby Coleshill House. With this initial strong lead, investigations start by looking into this house at The National Archives in London. Some of the files relating to secret organisations during the Second World War are generally declassified after 30 years and are held there.

Above the door of Mabel's post office, which has since been used as a shop, is a town council brown plaque commemorating Mabel's life. It describes the old post office as 'The Auxiliary Units Gateway'. During the war, a small post office such as this would have housed the telephone exchange and was also where ration books were issued. The Highworth post office changed location shortly after the war and initially very little of the premises as a wartime post office

can be seen. Further research, however, does confirm that the old post office was the contact address for Coleshill House.

The People's War website is a rich source of information and a great place to find individuals and associations associated with the Second World War. President of the Highworth Historical Society, Graham Tanner, and a teenager during the war in Highworth is the first person to be tracked down and contacted. He remembers how Mabel was still very Victorian in her approach to life and authoritarian. He also has a German publication showing the intended landing areas on the south coast for the invasion of Britain, which was originally handed out to the German troops.

After the fall of France in June 1940, Hitler ordered his Generals to organise the invasion of Britain. The plan was given the name 'Operation Sealion' and the objective was to land hundreds of thousands of German soldiers along the southeast coast of England. From the coast the German forces would have pushed toward the Midlands (Britain's industrial capital at the time) bringing them into the area around

Highworth. It is no surprise therefore that Churchill chose the area as the focus of his civilian-based resistance movement.

The investigations then shift focus to Coleshill, which is a tiny village compared to Highworth and is surrounded by a lot of farmland. Coleshill House was the nerve centre of British resistance during World War II. Civilians recruited for training would arrive first at Highworth post office, a decoy address. Mabel would then arrange for them to be transported to Coleshill. But the question is, did her involvement go any further than this? Speculation suggests that she was also involved in the actual spy training, but was she?

There are still underground operational bases in the grounds of Coleshill. The hideouts were built underground and were strategically situated up and down the country and provided a secure base from which the Auxiliary Units could plan and act out their guerrilla tactics in the event of a German invasion. These operational bases could accommodate a patrol of around eight to ten personnel. The whole idea of this secret organisation

was that nobody else knew anything about it, except the patrol members. Not even their close family would have known. If the enemy had arrived they would have a code word. If received, they would converge at their operational base and disappear from the community. Their mission: to hamper the advance of an occupying German

BELOW The interior of one such OB at Coleshill House where up to seven operatives would live for up to a fortnight along with provisions and weaponry

THE POST MISTRESS WHO WAS A SPY

force.

Unfortunately Coleshill House burned down in 1952 and the only thing left is a box hedge that marks the perimeter of where the house once stood, plus some outbuildings. Of course, this doesn't help much with the task of recreating a picture of how things once looked! With only a few carved stones left of the original house, the help of the National Monuments Record in Swindon is required to find more detailed plans and photographs.

The house was, in fact, an impressive Cromwellian stately home built between 1649 and 1662 by a student of Inigo Jones, the famous architect who designed Covent Garden. By drawing out the plan of the house from these documents, a sunken room that leads to another series of rooms that are not underneath the main block of the house, but are beyond the house itself are discovered. Actually going back to the site to see if these extra subterranean rooms still exist proves to be correct and an entrance to an underground room is found. The existence of an iron bar proves that it must have been used in the 20th century.

The question still remains, however, how did Mabel fit into all of this? From the archives

it is uncovered that she worked at the post office from 1916 in fact, which puts her in the right place at the right time. Also found is a top-secret document that details the work of the Auxiliary Units based at Coleshill, which is where the signals unit was based. They would have been in charge of coordinating all the activities up and down the country as and when the German's moved inland. The definitive link between Highworth and Coleshill is also made.

ABOVE Part of Coleshill Estate

Finding a surviving Auxiliary Unit member and getting a first-hand account of events is of course fantastic for investigations and he was certainly aware of Mabel. According to him, however, she was not a spy or involved in the training. She was just the postmistress who didn't ask awkward questions. The Mable fable, as he called it, is just a fabricated story that has become very elaborated over the years. She was merely the gateway from Highworth to Coleshill and that's all her role ever was.

One final question still remains, however. Was Mabel on Hitler's hit list? Hitler's hit list can be found at the Imperial War Museum and it documents all the people, places and institutions that would have been eradicated if Germany had occupied Britain. Mabel Stranks is not listed, whereas Chamberlain and Churchill unsurprisingly are!

Chapter 8

Murder at Berkeley Castle

The mystery surrounding the death of one of England's last court jesters, a Mr Dicky Pearce, who died at Berkeley Castle in Gloucestershire in 1725 is the subject of our next Mystery of Britain. Was his death an accident, brought on by natural causes, or could he have been murdered?

Berkeley Castle has been home to the Berkeley family for over 850 years. Although the original fortifications are long gone, the site dates back over 1,000 years to Anglo Saxon times. The castle was the scene of a royal murder and even got a name check in Shakespeare's play Richard II.

Initiated by Charles Berkeley himself, the quest is to find out the truth and circumstances surrounding the death of the last court jester. Charles Berkeley would like to find out why the Earl of Suffolk's jester Dicky Pearce came to Berkeley. He fell to his death, but was he pushed? Was there an ulterior motive? Charles would also like to know what the Great Hall would have looked like and what went on there on the night of Pearce's death.

The family myth is that Charles' ancestor, the third Earl of Berkeley, was holding a banquet one evening in 1725. The Great Hall was filled with distinguished guests including the Earl of Suffolk who had brought his jester to entertain everyone. The poor man fell to his death that evening inside the

Great Hall from the Minstrels' Gallery. No one knows after 250 years if this was a terrible accident or a murder; or even if it is all just a myth.

The first task at the archives is to search for any documentation relating to Pearce's death or the events of that fateful evening in 1725. With no coroner's report evident, newspaper archives have to be looked at in order to, if possible, find his obituary instead. The precise date of his burial is recorded as the 18th June 1725, but the Gloucester Journal, that covers the period in question, doesn't contain anything about Dicky, or his death or his burial.

The castle archives are the next port of call and last resort if any light is to be shed on the mystery of Dicky Pearce. Records of payment for his jester services are interrogated, but no hard evidence is found. Even the castle archivist doesn't think there is anything there about Dicky specifically. The majority of the records stored in

ABOVE Berkeley Castle

FAR LEFT Depiction of a jester by William Merritt Chase

the archive are to do with the management of the estate; it is a business and not personal archive. Although personal records from ancestors may have existed, later generations systematically destroyed evidence in order to keep the family name and reputation in tact.

The search also begins with regard to evidence about the personality and role in society that Pearce may have had at the time. Interviewing a modern day jester, who is a member of The National Guild of Jesters, is a natural place to start. Having researched the history of his trade, it turns out that Dicky Pearce is still a bit of a celebrity in jesting circles and the belief is that he was a dwarf or an 'unfortunate'.

One would assume that finding the correct grave would also help mat-

BELOW Example of a Great Hall in a castle (Doune Castle Scotland)

ters, but two anomalies come up with regard to the grave of Dicky Pearce, however. The engraving in stone states that he died in 1725 at the age of 63, but the design of the tomb doesn't fit with the style of that period, but is from a much later period and has the date 1822 on the other side. Why would a tomb be erected 100 years after his death?

By examining other pictures of Berkeley Castle in the local area it also becomes apparent that the castle has had a major makeover. Perhaps the clues to Dicky's death lie, not in the stories told, but in the building itself. A castle such as Berkeley would very rarely have been built in one go; successive owners would have added extensions, revamped parts to keep up with the latest fashions and even knocking earlier sections down. These findings naturally instigate the task of investigating the Great Hall.

The story has always been that the jester was performing above the dining guests on the Minstrels' gallery when he fell or was pushed to his death. But when looking at the Great Hall it is agreed that for a jester to perform from the gallery wouldn't make sense, as the guests would not have been able to see or interact with him up there. If the outside of the castle has changed so much over the years, maybe the inside of the Great Hall

could have also been altered significantly.

The gallery or screen that Dicky Pearce was supposed to have performed on turns out to be Elizabethan, dating to around 1560 to 1580. At the bottom of one of the decorative panel's is a dragon with its head chopped off. It is therefore suspected that the screen was once bigger than it is now and was cut down to fit the size of Berkeley's Great Hall, having come from somewhere else. There is, however, no doubt that the hall is medieval in origin, but the closer certain features are looked at, the less is believed in their authenticity. With these revelations now uncovered, it is more likely that someone intentionally wanted to create an image of the past in a much more recent period.

With the aid of an engraving of the Great Hall from the castle archives there is enough to create a visual image of how it would have really looked. This image has no screen/gallery at the end of the hall. A 1663 inventory of the hall also states that the space consisted of two tables, a couple of benches, 12 leather chairs and nothing else to report. Of course in the space of 200 years anything is possible, although it is thought that by the time Dicky Pearce was supposed to have been there in 1725 the Great Hall was still without the gallery and screen.

Another picture of the Great Hall is located in the castle shop. Titled as the Dining Room, the image dates back to early to mid-Victorian, a century after the jester's time. Although the hall could have been changed in that century, the picture shows some big differences and so much more compared to the Great Hall as it is now.

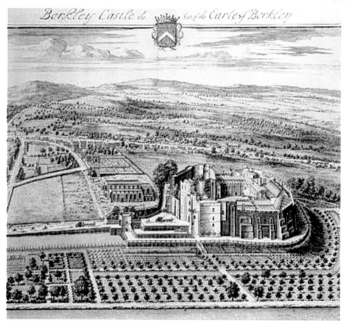

FAR RIGHT Example of a Court Jester

One theory is that the grave is from 1822 and the hall is a more modern fabrication. It is therefore possible that the family could have invented the entire legend in the early 19th century,

probably based on a real person, but they made it up to increase the tourist trade visiting the castle.

There is no doubt that the story has been absolutely fundamental to the survival of the Berkeley family over the centuries. It also looks like there was an enormous amount of illegitimacy going on in the 1780s and 1790s. The Berkeley family were hauled through the courts on several occasions due to one illegitimate son, William Fitzhardinge, trying to claim rights to the estate as a legitimate heir. At a time when the family's heritage was in dispute, it is probable that the Dicky Pearce story was fabricated to help fire the public's imagination. The new tourist trade would have helped cover the legal costs during that difficult time, and visitors to the castle would link the 19th-century branch of the Berkeley family with their revered ancestors.

Chapter 9

The Hunt for the Lost Railway

In Darlington, the birthplace of the railways, the next Mystery of Britain goes back in time to that pioneering age of steam, the Victorian era. Darlington in County Durham is the home of the railways and in 1825 the first passenger steam railway opened, running between Stockton and Darlington.

In 1910, a granite obelisk was erected in memory of local railwayman John Lamb from the nearby station in Ferryhill. An engine driver and chairman of the local council, the obelisk was put up in his honour shortly after his death. The local toyshop owner has been looking into his family history and wants to investigate to discover if John Lamb was his great grandfather.

As the Victorian transport revolution began it turned Britain into the world's first railway nation. By 1852 a skeleton of tracks was already in place enabling countrywide travel. The railways changed society forever and opened up a world of new opportunities, such as commuting and seaside holidays. There was opposition to this, however, and the Duke of Wellington was incensed that working class people were suddenly mobile.

A closer look at the monument is obviously required to try and gather evidence. The first thing that is striking is that because it is made from granite, not the local sandstone, the obelisk would have had to have travelled to

ABOVE An Old Coal
Train

Darlington. The name of the sculptor from Hartlepool is also on the memorial. Ironically, it is thought that the stone would have travelled by sea and not by train!

Ferryhill station was where John Lamb apparently spent most of his working life. It was once a thriving railway complex, with a station, marshalling yard and sheds. Although little remains of the site now, in its day a million tonnes of coal a year would have passed through Darlington and this industry brought wealth to the area. Looking at a picture of the site from the 1920s it is very clear just how

BELOW Darlington station, opened July 1st 1887

built up and thriving the industry once was.

Ferryhill station opened in 1839 and five years later it was a stop off on the main London to Edinburgh route. By 1863, 140 trains passed through the station every day, carrying passengers as well as freight such as road stone, coal and fish. In 1913, the north eastern railway network had 500 stations and issued nearly 60 million 3rd class tickets. In 1967, however, Ferryhill station closed and there is not much left of it now. By piecing together as much evidence as possible, a picture can of course be created of what it would have looked like when John Lamb worked there in the 1890s.

Again, speaking to local historians, journalists and first hand witnesses to

BELOW Darlington station, opened July 1st 1887

events is a brilliant help when trying to solve mysteries such as this. In this particular instance a local journalist from the Northern Echo had written a few articles about John Lamb in the past. He provides a photo of him, some family tree research, and looking through the old newspapers it details the events of his death. Would you believe that he died by choking on a mutton bone?!

At the Darlington station museum archives it is also possible to dig deeper into John Lamb's family history. The newspaper obituary is useful, but something more official is required; a birth certificate for example.

In view of the fact that the museum was also Darlington station, it is the perfect place to dig up some more evidence to help solve the mystery and also to find out more about what John Lamb's life would have been like as an engine driver.

On a typical journey from Newcastle to Edinburgh (about 100 miles) four to five tonnes of coal would have to be shovelled by the fireman – a very demanding and not glamorous job.

ABOVE LEFT A painting of Stockton and Darlington Railway

ABOVE RIGHT Driver and Fireman on Steam Locomotive

The front part of the driver's body would be roasting from the furnace and the back half would have been totally exposed to the elements. They were known, however, to knock up a cooked breakfast by putting the bacon and eggs on the shovel and cooking it over the furnace!

To reach the esteemed rank of engine driver would have taken many years. Initially they would have been engine cleaners, then firemen and eventually

drivers. They could have been firemen for 20 or 30 years before becoming a driver, and then it depended on dead men's shoes. As a skilled job, drivers also got paid an above average wage for an industrial worker.

From the museum archives some rare pieces of railway heritage linking in with John Lamb are found. His position of engine driver brought with it the privilege of a free train pass for life, albeit a third class one. The First

World War changed a lot of things and John Lamb's memorial was erected just before. It was, at that time, a very sentimental society. Victorian and Edwardian society would frequently present an award or memorial to someone for a lifetime's accomplishment in any field. This was therefore a very natural and normal thing to do in society at the time.

John Lamb died in quite tragic circumstances and he was a distinguished member of local society. A person didn't have to do anything that groundbreaking, it was an occasion that was marked in the way that society did it then. It was a lifetime of hard work initially as part of an exciting new technology engulfing the nation, and later serving his community as a councillor that earned John Lamb the obelisk.

Finally, at the museum archives the marriage certificate of Barrie Lamb's grandfather (George Herbert Lamb) is found, linking Barrie with John as his great grandfather. To cross check the findings George Herbert's birth records are also found, which gives the conclusive proof they have been looking for. A census record also supports both documents for John Lamb.

Chapter 10

The Man with Two Tombs

FAR RIGHT St Mary
Redcliffe Church, Bristol

Bristol in the 15th century was the second richest city in England and there is a very fishy tale from that very century that needs investigating. The Mystery of Britain here is to solve the case of a medieval trader who has two very different tombs in the same church. It is known that this was a very wealthy man, but he is also shown in the church in priest's robes. How can one man's body be buried in two different places?

The city of Bristol has been a thriving trading port since Roman times and one of its medieval shipping magnets is the subject of this particular mystery. A young chorister walks past the two tombs every week in the church of Saint Mary Redcliffe, and he is desperate to investigate this man, William Canynge, to find out exactly why this is the case.

Saint Mary Redcliffe Church is one of the most beautiful gothic churches in England and almost on the scale of a cathedral. Although the oldest parts are 12th century, most of the magnificent building was constructed during the 15th century. Mr William Canynge was in fact one of the church's main benefactors when it was built.

The tombs themselves are completely different. On one he appears as a wealthy merchant lying beside his wife, whilst the second one shows him as a simply dressed priest.

Two effigies of William II Canynges:

RIGHT in red velvet mayoral robes beside his wife Joan under an ornate stone canopy

FAR RIGHT Alabaster, in canonical vestments, moved from Collegiate Church of Westbury-on-Trym, Bristol following Dissolution

BELOW Effigy of Joan Burton(d.1467), wife of William II Canynges of Bristol. Church of St Mary Redcliffe, Bristol

The Latin inscription above the ornate tomb says 'pray for the souls of William Canynge and his wife Joanna'. The head of the tomb is a pillow held by two angels on either side and his wife lies next to him. Both look very happy and peaceful. On the base of the tomb is his distinctive coat of arms that shows three Moors' heads with dark skin, each wearing a headband of blue and white cloth; a logo representing his family. Without a doubt it is a rich merchant's tomb with all the trimmings, but the second one is totally the opposite.

Showing the man in priest's robes there is no paint on this tomb anywhere, unlike the first. Although two angels also hold up the head pillow there is a large bible underneath this one. They definitely look like they are statues of the same man, however.

The quest begins by way of tracking down documentary evidence about the Canynges, which begins at the local antiquarian bookshop. A local medieval historian is also found to interview and the inscriptions in the church also have to be studied.

Although written after his death, an inscription that is full of information about Canynge's life is found: he was a mayor five times and it also confirms that he went into the church. Very importantly, his exact date of death is recorded on the inscription

taken over and turned into a car showroom! The front of the house would have been on the street and at the back a grand tower would have made a statement to all. The only aspect that remains are the skeleton structures of grand stone arches that are thought to have been part of the Great Hall in the grand medieval house. Canynge was one of the richest men in Bristol at the time and it is thought that he even entertained King Edward IV at his home.

Needing to gather as much information as possible in order to paint a realistic visual picture of how Canynge's house would have looked, the opposite end of the building is investigated where the tower (that fronted onto the river) would have been. The very scant remains of the tower is actually on the side of a modern building, but it still shows early windows and the make-up of the tower walls.

An interview with a local historian reveals information about how

as 7th November 1474. In view of the fact that burials were not recorded in Parish records until the 1530s, this is a great piece of evidence.

Not forgetting the age we live in, useful and interesting information can of course also be found online. Following some online investigations it is discovered that there is a bit of Canynge's House still standing in Bristol. With the help of a city archaeologist and a visit to the actual site, it is discovered that it was demolished as late as 1937 when the whole site was

THE MAN WITH TWO TOMBS

Canynge came from a long line of merchants and was at least the third generation. The family before him had been cloth merchants, but Canynge diversified for the first time and moved into ships. Rather than take the risks of trying to buy and sell commodities, he leased out his ships for other merchants, and this is how he made his enormous fortune. Canynge would have been part of a very small and elite group of extremely wealthy merchants in Bristol at the time.

The evidence taken from the church naturally leads the investigation to the Bristol Record Office. With the date of Canynge's death confirmed, the search for his will can begin. In the process, many other documents about Canynge, particularly the last years of his life, including detailed records about the construction of the large painted tomb are also uncovered. His will also confirms that he had a very strong connection with the church. By 1474 he was acting as the Dean of Westbury, which is a church not far from Bristol. So he was, in fact, in place as a churchman at the time of his death. The documents also reveal that his wife, Joanna died in 1467 and was

buried in the large painted tomb. He went into the priesthood following the death of his beloved wife.

Also discovered is a chronicle written by the English chronicler William of Worcester, who came across Canynge's house and wrote down many details about it, including what it looked liked and its dimensions.

THE MAN WITH TWO TOMBS

With regard to his business, Canynge owned 10 ocean-going vessels that were half of the entire Bristol fleet. These ships were the super tankers of their day and were 26 metres long. A restoration is in fact underway of the only known surviving medieval ship that was discovered in the Severn Estuary in Newport in 2002.

Another chronicle about the lives of the mayors of Bristol in the mid-15th century is also found in the record office. The document goes to the very heart of the reason why Canynge had a double life – that of a wealthy merchant and that of a clergyman. It seems that he was being put under considerable pressure by the King to marry for a second time. So, within a year of his wife's death Canynge became a priest so that he could avoid such a fate. The rest of his family had already died

and he devoted himself to the church. By 1474 he was the Dean of Westbury.

Documents are also discovered that should solve the mystery of the two tombs. A piece of evidence from 1917 about Westbury Church states that Canynge's tomb originally stood in that church and was probably removed in the 16th century. Whilst many believe that the place of rest for Canynge's actual body is in the ornate tomb next to his wife, the theory that comes to light is that the Bishop of Westbury Church and Canynge were great friends. The Bishop wanted an effigy of his good friend to be placed next to his own tomb in that church. This was then later moved to Saint Mary Redcliffe. So in fact, Canynge only has one real tomb, but he does have two monuments.

LEFT Alabaster effigy of William II Canynges(d.1474) at St Mary Redcliffe Church, Bristol

Chapter 11

The Tower People of Shetland

On the far edge of Europe, a long, long time ago, a series of monumental stone towers, known as Brochs, once dominated the landscape. Situated on the Shetland Isles in Scotland the identity of the ancient people who once lived in the mysterious Broch towers is an intriguing mystery.

More than 100 of these strange and haunting structures were built on the Shetland Isles. It is time to discover more about these lost communities to find out how they lived and why they created these monumental buildings.

In the wet and windy, most northerly part of the British Isles, it is perhaps surprising to know that people have inhabited the region for over 5,000 years. At a site called Jarlshof there are remains of buildings from every period of Shetland history. There's a laird's house from the 17th century, and Viking remains go back to the 9th century. One structure, however, stands out from the rest and represents a remarkable flowering of Shetland civilisation. The remains of a massive Iron Age Broch is there, which dates back at least 2,000 years. The question is, how did an Iron Age community prosper sufficiently to build these monumental towers on the bleak and isolated island?

Investigations begin by travelling to the small island of Mousa to see the

ABOVE Dun Carloway Broch, Lewis, Scotland

most intact example remaining, aided by a Shetland archaeologist who has made a detailed study of the Brochs. Many archaeologists believe that after Stonehenge, Brochs are the most significant prehistoric architecture in Great Britain.

To enter the middle of the Broch one walks through about five metres of solid wall, and above the doorway height the walls become double skinned, having an inner and outer. Architecturally it is built in a very sophisticated way, so they certainly

ABOVE Broch of Mousa - interior

rey, the thick base gives way to double walls and sandwiched between them is a staircase. Within the wall at the base are entrances to a number of cells or chambers. Here another advanced technique was used known as 'corbelling' to create a domed ceiling that would support the weight above. This was most certainly an ambitious building for the Iron Age.

Ledges around the inner wall suggest what the inside of a Broch may have looked like – several levels of private rooms surrounding a central courtyard. It is possible that it could have been home to a large group of people who would have been well protected from the harsh weather conditions.

The Brochs that are known about were all built along the coast of the islands and there are a further 40 that are likely to be found. All the Brochs were built in strategic locations and from the air most look like they were built for defence, and some even have extra outer walls. They are also quite close together, so it would certainly have been possible for messages to be sent between them. Many think that defence was a part of their reason, but

knew what they were doing and had a vision for what the end design was going to be. The entire structure would have been crafted from carefully made sandstone blocks. Above the first sto-

due to their large imposing nature, they would also have been a great deterrent to anyone arriving by sea, as a sign that people should not land there. It has been suggested that they would have been defending their territory against the Romans coming as slave traders. Others have suggested that the impact of the Romans had sent shockwaves up the country that there was unrest further south.

The sheer number and size of the Brochs also suggests a large population, perhaps as many as the 23,000 that live in Shetland today. But how did they earn a living to enable them to build such grand structures?

On the edge of Shetland airport another Broch remain has been uncovered; a giant one, a major settlement. Here the Broch was surrounded by a number of circular dwellings called 'wheel houses'. This site is the first to be thoroughly investigated and is now one of the most important archaeological sites in Britain. The artefacts found and being recovered could help reveal the secret of the success of the Broch people and how they lived, including how they fed themselves. The grain found during the dig is also very useful

to the archaeologists and should help to identify exactly when the Broch was first built. Knowing when may be a further clue to why they were built in the first place.

Although the landscape of the Shetland

LEFT Approximate locations of the brochs in Scotland

Isles looks unsustainable for growing grain, perhaps the landscape was different during the Iron Age? From pollen analysis, it is known in fact that Shetland was covered in low woodland trees including rowan, willow, hazel and birch. Before the Iron Age, however, settlers started cutting down the trees and at the same time the climate grew colder and damper. This encouraged the growth of mosses, heathers

ABOVE Jarlshof, Shetland, Scotland - aisled roundhouse and broch

etc. that created a build up of peat. By the Iron Age there would have been very little woodland left.

There are some stretches along the coast, however, that have well cultivated fields where the soil is less peaty and therefore less acidic. There is also a lot of shell sand around the coast, which if put on the fields also helps to neutralise the soil. With confirmation from the excavation site that they also used animal manure, it is quite likely

LEFT Oats and and Potatoes Growing in Shetland

that the Broch dwellers could have grown plenty of grain on the lowlands.

With animals on the higher ground and grain growing on the lower, the only aspect left is to find out how they utilised the sea surrounding them. The excavation teams have found many little fishbone remains such as saithes or piltocks. The evidence suggests that they were easily caught along the coast by dragging a lure and hook through the water.

Although the Broch people had a plentiful supply of food, that on its own is not enough to sustain such a society; they must have had further resources to live. At a soapstone or Steatite quarry that was quarried in Viking times there is evidence of activity where pots have been cut straight out of the rock and the shapes are still left where domestic vessels were carved out. There is also evidence that suggests that the people of the Iron Age were also taking advantage of this technique. Not only is the stone soft, so quite simple to quarry, it is also easy to carve into shapes using the correct technique. It seems that the Broch people were skilled at working mineral resources of different types, including copper and bronze.

In fact, metalwork was also an important part of their lives, and the evidence from the excavation site includes copper moulds, hammer scale and crucibles. It also becomes apparent that the ready supply of peat was also

RIGHT Remains of a spiral staircase in the Broch

FAR RIGHT Broch Interior

a vital resource as fuel during the Iron Age, just as it has remained for the last 2,000 years. They would have used it for cooking and heating their homes, and it would also have led to the development of metalworking. Casting and forging metal, particularly using bronze, appears to have been prevalent. This also means that they had to trade with Cornwall that had tin depositaries to mix with their Shetland copper.

It is now evident how the Broch people prospered. They could feed themselves well, they had access to ample raw materials, and they had the skills to use them. It is even likely that they were trading with Cornwall nearly 1,000 miles away. And when were the Brochs built? Well the date 800-400 B.C. from the foundations has been determined, with the date above the foundations put at around 400-200 B.C.

Following these investigations, the notion of them building against a Roman invasion does not in fact now make sense, as they were building 300 years before the Romans. They were more likely to be the centre of wealth – a village, surrounded by much smaller dwellings, with the inhabitants of the Brochs being the gentry of their time.

Chapter 12

The Abandoned Marsh

On the bleak Romney Marsh, at the extreme south east of Britain, there are few signs of habitation. Look carefully, however, and there are clues that reveal this part of England was not always so deserted; abandoned buildings stand in the middle of fields. There are tales of towns drowned at sea, and all around there is evidence of a forgotten past. It is time to unravel the mystery of this haunting and empty landscape.

The landscape looks timeless, and somehow it's hard to imagine how Romney Marsh ever looked anything other than tranquil yet deserted. But with the many ruins scattered around the area, a medieval church for exam-ple that must have had a congrega-tion at some time, begs the question about when these communities did inhabit the area, and what drove them all away? Was there a drama or disas-ter that befell the people of Romney Marsh?

Evidence is still emerging with regard to the settlements that once dotted the marsh. Digging at a quarry near the town of Lydd is revealing signs of early occupation. The archae-ologists have been there since 1991 and they have already covered a large landmass during their investigations. In marshland such as Romney, the most obvious sign of occupation is with the presence of drainage ditches.

ABOVE Drainage Ditch on Romney Marsh

Drainage ditches are vital for any settlement on the marshes. Hardly above sea level, the whole area would flood very quickly if it wasn't constantly drained. As water comes off the fields it can be routed and controlled as it flows through a network of ditches. It is then fed out into bigger channels that carry the water onwards towards the sea.

The part of the south coast from Hythe to Winchelsea was drained and reclaimed from the sea, turning unusable salt marsh into productive farm-

fairly inhospitable conditions of the area, compared to the larger towns, the reason people started moving to the marshes was simply due to the pressure of population. From 1100 onwards the population of England was increasing and people needed new land, so they came down from the hills and found around 50 square miles of it, albeit land that needed draining!

Of course there were also several important shipping ports on the south coast, which meant that moving to the marshes was also good for trading and commerce. During the 12th and 13th centuries, therefore, the marshes were turned into successful farming settlements. It was the beginning of the distinct and beautiful landscape that still exists there today.

The whole history of how the marshes came to exist in the first place is related to the power of the sea and what it did over thousands of years, changing the shape and position of the

land. But it appears to be the most southern part of the region that has suffered most from whatever tragedy overtook the people who once lived there.

Since the 9th century the Priory at Canterbury had owned the marshes. The cathedral archives will hopefully reveal vital information to find out when the southern part was first drained. A document that dates from 1152 to 1167 that gives evidence of the beginning of life on the marshes is found. Bearing in mind the harsh and

coast. The shingle bank barrier that runs along the coast is always on the move. It becomes clear that the protection of a shingle bank must have always been vital to the survival of the communities. In the 21st century it is maintained by diggers constantly moving shingle to ensure the barrier always exists. It must have been much harder to maintain during the 13th century and would have been very vulnerable during bad weather.

During the 13th century the sea did break the shingle barrier and flooded several miles inland of the marsh. The land was abandoned and reverted back to salt marsh for 200 to 300 years. Five miles inland a reinforced wall was built, as the danger of flooding became widely accepted. It was this wall that stopped the sea flooding any further inland. People living on the flooded land would have been driven back to the other side of the wall or up onto the Weald of Kent.

The succession of storms in the late 1200s had a dramatic effect on many of the (what were once busy and thriving) ports on the south coast, and many were just gobbled up by the sea. Old Winchelsea was one of these, and

ABOVE Example of a Modern Sea Wall

New Winchelsea was therefore built to house people dispersed by the floods. It is a good example of a 13th century new town. It became a major port specialising in the wine trade and 50 medieval wine vaults can still be identified. The port of New Winchelsea is no more, however, as the River Brede silted up and the town gradually failed as it relied on the river for its trade. In its heyday, the port had 82 separate private wharves with boats of over 200 tonnes mooring there. This was one of the major three ports of England in naval terms. The town's prosperity only in fact lasted for about 60 years before this happened. To top it all, the Black Death then hit the town, which was the final straw. Following that, nearly half of all the dwellings lay empty.

Today, Winchelsea is about one-third of its original size. Trees mark the boundary of the medieval port, first rebuilt on the hill, then deserted by the sea, then finally struck by disease.

Of course the Black Death spread through Romney Marshes as it did through the rest of the country. The evidence for this comes from the deaths of the clergy, the only group for whom records survive. It could be argued that the poor people of the marshes were struck by disasters of almost biblical proportions. With floods and plagues, it is understandable why some churches lost their congregations!

Following the 13th-century marsh flooding, when did things improve on the marsh after that and the plague? The area originally flooded up to the wall, which remained so well into the 15th century and became a salt marsh. Finally, at the end of the 15th and beginning of the 16th century embankments were built and the land was reclaimed. When they reclaimed it, however, they did it in a totally different way. The land was divided into large fields where they were able to graze sheep. Having sheep there rather than people meant that the land needed far less manpower to manage it – a shepherd would have looked after quite a large area of land. That was the start of the Romney Marsh sheep industry. There are still little huts on the land that the shepherds would have lived in during the lambing season.

So, for hundreds of years the landscape took on a very different appearance. Dominated by sheep, they were there long enough for a specific breed to develop over centuries – the Romney sheep.

Although it seemed that the people had at last tamed the land, the population never recovered. The new threat now facing the people of Romney Marsh was malaria carried by mosquitos, and it wreaked havoc on the marshland populations. It seems that from the early 17th century mortality begins to peak, and of course people suffered from all sorts of other diseases as well. Malaria really was the final straw for the marshland population.

Built for defence in the early 19th century, the cutting of the Royal Military Canal was the real turning point, and it became the most important drainage channel to the sea. By the end of the century the mosquitos and the malaria had gone but the population never recovered.

Chapter 13

Britain Before the Ice

On the Gower Peninsula in Paviland, South Wales, there is a spectacular landscape of cliffs and caves. In 1823, in one of these caves a skeleton was found surrounded by beautiful artefacts of ivory and shell. It is famously known as the 'Red Lady of Paviland', but it turned out to be a young man who died around 29,000 years ago. His burial can give us a glimpse of a world that existed before the height of the Ice Age. Just a few thousand years after his death, ice sheets spread south across Britain. It is time to unravel the mystery of the lost world in which this man lived. How would the country have looked 29,000 years ago when the young man's body was buried in the cave?

The landscape that we are surrounded by now has all developed over the last 10,000 years since the great ice sheet retreated. Before the ice advanced, however, there was a different Britain in which people lived with a landscape that has long since vanished as the ice obliterated it.

Before the ice, the sea would have been about 70 miles west of the Gower Peninsula. Since then, as the ice melted, the sea has risen by about 120 metres.

The remains of the body are now kept in Oxford. It was geologist William Buckland, Professor of Geology at Oxford University, who first examined the bones in 1823 and he labelled them as female and was struck by their covering of red dye, what he called 'ruddle'.

It is estimated that the man was about 5' 10", so quite a tall, long legged, long armed member of our own species, compared with the more short, stocky Neanderthals. The more heavily built Neanderthals are known to have survived until about this time, and although not the entire skeleton of the young man survived, there is enough to show that this man was quite different. He is, in fact, the first known modern human in Britain. They also know that he was a hunter, as beautifully crafted flint spearheads were found near the body.

Also found with the body was the skull of a mammoth. It indicates that this was an exceptional burial for an exceptional person. Polished fragments of mammoth ivory, also painted in red dye were found that are thought to be associated with magic and spirituality. This implies that he could have been a medicine man perhaps, or someone who could communicate with the spirit world and was therefore important to his society.

ABOVE A Mammoth
Skull

FAR RIGHT Cathole
Cave

These people had strong beliefs and elaborate rituals, and it appears to have been a complex and well-organised community. But what was life like for these people?

A good place to start trying to answer these questions is by investigating the record of climate change over the years. Evidence of this can often be found in caves so in the nearby Cathole Cave stalagmites are sought. Stalagmites and stalactites only grow during warmer climate spells. This is because if the ground above is frozen there will be no water

coming down into the caves. Also, when it is cold there is not enough biological activity and the carbonic acid doesn't exist to dissolve the limestone, which deposits the stalagmites.

Because the growth of cave formations depends on climate, they preserve a climate record dating back thousands of years. Caves in the area have been examined and samples taken for analysis, from which climate changes can be identified and dated depending on the formation of the rocks when cross-sectioned. From the stalagmites in the caves, it seems that when the young man was buried it was getting significantly colder; the ice was on its way. Within a few thousand years of the young man's burial the entire area to the north of the cave would have been buried under hundreds of metres of ice.

To find out what the landscape would have been like 29,000 years ago, the help of a paleobiologist at the University of Birmingham is enlisted, who has been trying to identify the remains of insects found in sediments from around the country. The kind of insects living in Britain that many years ago that have been identified are mainly beetles, which tend to survive because of their hard outer shells. The beetles can actually be matched up with living species of today, but many of them are species adapted to cold climates and no longer occur in Britain. The most common dung beetle from 29,000 years ago is in fact only now found in Tibet! What this suggests is that the climate all those years ago was something like the Arctic Siberian climate of present time.

The landscape would have been totally treeless and with very small

amounts of vegetation. It would have looked completely different to how it does today. With the sea 70 miles away, there would have just been a vast expanse of tundra, a few small

trees, low bushes, and some grasses. This begs the question therefore of how the people of Paviland survived with so little vegetation.

They were in fact hunters, and the caves also hold the clues to what animals were in existence at this time. The bones that have been found preserved in the sediments prove what pre-Ice Age mammals existed, and include: the woolly mammoth, the woolly rhinoceros, reindeer, horses, bears and spotted hyenas.

To find out exactly what their diet consisted of, however, the help of a bioarchaeologist at Bradford University is required. By analysing minute quantities of early human and Neanderthal bones it is possible to identify what they ate 29,000 years ago and how the two compare. It certainly puts the phrase 'we are what we eat' into perspective!

From the research it appears that Neanderthals were 100% meat eaters. The diet of our man, The Red Lady, compares more closely with animals like the bear, which suggests that as much as 15-20% of the protein in the bones was fish or other seafood. The diets of the first modern humans were therefore quite different from the Neanderthals. This versatility in diet and ability to be creative with food is the marked difference between the two and would have given the early humans the upper hand when it came to survival, particularly as the climate got colder.

Bearing in mind how far away the sea was, the Paviland people must have travelled for food, which suggests that they would have spent quite a lot of time by the sea. They were most likely part-nomadic people and would have moved inland to search for other sources of food.

In view of the fact that the Gower Peninsula was still part of mainland Europe at that time, it is perhaps little surprise that similar people lived right across the continent, from the cave at Paviland to Siberia. Their burial patterns are strikingly alike: the remains are all covered in red dye and accompanied by elaborate shell decorations and mammoth ivory jewellery; and they have flint spearheads and stone tools beside them.

Other European sites have shed light on the history of Britain before the Ice Age and include evidence of shelters, sophisticated stone tools, basketry, textiles, and beautiful jewellery. It seems that there would have been a remarkable sense of community 29,000 years ago.

BELOW Typical Neanderthal Burial

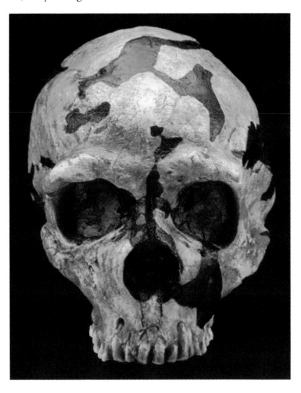

Chapter 14

Secrets of the Flood

In the Solent, off the south coast of England, low tide is a very special time, when secrets are uncovered that are otherwise hidden beneath the waves. Just east of Portsmouth, Stone Age axes and Roman pottery can be found at low tide just lying in the mud. Could people have once been living in a landscape that is now covered by the sea? What caused the area to be flooded?

The most recent find in the Solent is in Langstone harbour and is that of a hollowed out log boat bedded in the mud. A piece of the timber was taken for carbon dating and it has been aged between 410 A.D. and 460 A.D., which means it is a Saxon boat. In addition to this boat, other remarkable traces of wood have been found and it turns out that they could possibly be the remains of sheep pens. It seems that 1,500 years ago people were farming on a site that is now just a stretch of tidal mud. This naturally begs the question as to when this area became flooded.

Local archaeologists have found another line of posts from the same period in a different area, Wootton-Quarr, which shows evidence of some major medieval construction. A range of objects has also been found in the same area from totally different periods of history – a Viking-age pin and an early 17th-century shoe for example. The pin was found closer to the sea,

ABOVE Langstone Harbour

and even further from the shore was a much older Roman dish. It seems that the further you go out, the older the objects are. The very earliest finds that have been made on the beach include arrowheads that are around 5,000 years old.

It seems that the sea has been flooding the beach gradually over thousands of years. Six hundred years ago medieval people built timber structures, 2,000 years ago remains of Roman jetties have been found closer to the sea, and 5,000 years ago Neolithic people

LEFT An ancient oak tree

FAR LEFT Early stone tools

were building wooden track ways, of which remains are hundreds of metres from the present coastline. There is also evidence, right at the water's edge, of what looks like the remains of an ancient forest.

To discover just how far these remains go into the Solent, divers have explored an area off the northwest coast of the Isle of Wight. Marine archaeologists have collected samples from this submerged forest and some of the trees measure 14 or 15 metres long. They are most certainly forest trees! One specimen of oak tree dates back about 8,400 years and is extremely well preserved.

As well as trees, the divers have found other evidence, including flint tools that indicate human occupation at one time. The peat deposits in which these artefacts are buried date back some 8,200 years. It appears that the deeper the divers dive, the further back

in time they go.

It seems that as time went on these people had to progressively move further inland as the water rose. Was the flooding process slow and progressive, or was the area affected by anything meteorologically devastating?

Marine biologists have also taken core sediment samples from the bottom of the sea that have been analysed at Southampton University with the aim of discovering at what time the water started coming in. The bottom of the sample represents the oldest part (about 8,500 years old) and changes can be identified moving up the sample.

The evidence shows that just over 8,000 years ago the Solent would have been covered in a forest of oak trees and hunters could have walked across to what is now the Isle of Wight. Further up the sample the sediment changes to silty clay that is clearly salt marsh deposit. This indicates that over just a few hundred years the oak forest must have been gradually submerged in a flood and salt marsh took over. This would have driven people further inland and was the beginnings of the Solent landscape as we recognise it today.

The explanation for this first episode of flooding can be explained by the thawing of ice that caused many great floods at the time, but it doesn't explain why the sea kept rising over thousands of years.

500 miles away in Stirling in Scotland, a sea level change expert is able to shed light on this mystery. In the Stirling area, 9,000 years ago, the sea was present on what is now fertile farmland. The theory, which was originally a crucial insight into the mysteries of sea level change and now proven correct, is that the land moved up as opposed to the sea levels falling.

LEFT Solent Salt Marshes

RIGHT Solent Sea
Defences

The science behind the theory lies in the fact that when the land was covered in ice, the massive weight of it pushed the crust of the land down into softer rock that flowed away. When the ice melted the pressure was reduced, the softer rock flowed back and the land slowly rose.

So, whilst the Solent was flooding, Scotland was rising out of the sea. What is the connection? A map of the coverage and thickness of the ice over the United Kingdom some 22,000 years ago shows that the ice sheet was at its thickest on the west coast of Scotland, and there was no ice over the south of Britain.

It wasn't, in fact, just Scotland where the land moved. The huge weight of ice pushed Scotland down but tilted the southern end of Britain upwards. When the ice melted as the climate grew warmer the reverse happened – Scotland started rising and southern Britain sank back down. Geologists call it 'glacial rebound'.

This explains exactly what happened in the Solent. Following the initial great flood caused by the great ice thaw, the land actually started sinking, allowing the sea to continually rise over many years, and as salt water plants took over at the water's edge, so the salt marshes developed. The salt marsh then gradually moved inland. The salt marshes at Quay Haven in Swanwick are in fact identical to the salt marshes that developed all those years ago.

As people were forced to move progressively inland, the salt marsh would have been invaluable, serving as a protective barrier against tidal surges and storms. They would have also been the access roads to the sea for fishing and fowling. The marsh, in fact, is still advancing inland and researchers know that the land is sinking at a rate of approximately 1mm per year as the glacial rebound continues even after thousands of years. In addition, there is now global warming, also causing the sea levels to rise. In the last 2,000 years sea levels only rose by about 2 metres, so if the predictions are correct and sea levels rise in the Solent area by about half a metre in the next 100 years, there will be a rapid rise, five times faster than in the past. It is possible, therefore, that in a century or two, some of the dwellings and communities that have been built along the south coast, may in fact be flooded and could disappear.

Chapter 15

In Search of Irish Gold

The ancient landscape of Ireland is steeped in myths and legends. With some dating back 3,000 years to the time of its Bronze Age people, who left behind hoards of extraordinary artefacts made out of gold. It is a mystery, however, as to where they found the precious metal to work with. Was there a secret source of Bronze Age gold somewhere hidden within the landscape? A hidden mine? The time has come to try and shed light on this remarkable lost Eldorado.

In 1854, at a place called Mooghaun, a railway was excavated between Limerick and Ennis. Whilst digging, the workers found something quite extraordinary – a box containing a fantastic hoard of solid gold treasure including necklaces and bracelets. Unsurprisingly some disappeared, but some survived and this is a good example of many such hoards of gold that have been found all over Ireland.

It is not clear why so many Bronze Age people buried so much gold, although many believe that they were offerings to the gods. The collection of ancient Irish gold, held at the National Museum of Ireland in Dublin, is spectacular.

The Wicklow Hills became famous for a gold rush in the 1790s. This happened near the small town of Avoca, also better known as Ballykissangel from the popular television series.

ABOVE National Museum of Ireland

There is no reason why the Bronze Age people wouldn't have also found gold here if it was discovered in quantity during the late 18th century.

Gold is usually deep underground and has to be mined for, but sometimes the veins come to the surface and outcrops can appear, often where the gold is visible. As the outcrops wear and stones and pebbles get into streams, stream-based deposits then form. It is perfectly possible that the Bronze Age people would have had the technology of using a wooden frame and sheepskin to get it, using the fibres of the wool to trap the gold.

With the wooden frame (sheepskin placed on top) secured in the water, and a swift current running over it, the water would send the gold over the top where it would get trapped in the wool. The sheepskin would then be rolled up to secure any gold caught. The contents of the wool

would then be washed into a pan and carefully swirled around in the shallows to separate the light material from anything heavy, leaving any gold glistening in the bottom.

It is not certain, however, that the Bronze Age people would have ever found enough gold to make the type of objects held at the museum, from the (since named) Gold Mines River. To make the large pieces of finery that they did, they would have needed much larger deposits of gold, which they would have melted down to form bigger nuggets to sculpture into their desired items.

The composition of the gold artefacts is like a fingerprint that could, in theory, lead back to the source of the metal. A project working with that concept is already underway to measure the percentage of silver in the ancient objects in Dublin. This will then be compared with the gold that can still be found in the landscape.

Researchers have been taking samples from other sites in Ireland in addition to Wicklow. One of them, Croagh Patrick, is on the very west coast and is known as the holy mountain of Ireland. Once a year, bare-

ABOVE Croagh Patric

footed pilgrims walk to the church located on its summit. Wicklow gold samples have also been analysed and so far no match has been made between that and the Bronze Age samples. It is hoped that the gold on Croagh Patrick will lead to something.

Gold would have been found in this area in an outcrop of quartz on the mountainside for example. Within the quartz are areas that look a little brown or biscuit coloured, i.e. iron staining. This shows that there was some iron pyrites there, to which gold is associated. Through a magnifying glass, tiny bits of gold can be seen in the middle of the porous quartz.

Of course, the gold has to be extracted from the rock. Bronze Age man would have had a great deal of

ABOVE Quartz Outcrop

ing fire and water, this is a technique that the Bronze Age people would have been capable of implementing.

Although it is possible that there would have been a lot more gold at Croagh Patrick during the Bronze Age, geologists are still not convinced that it would have been enough to produce the large heavy items held in Dublin. They also wouldn't have had the technology to mine deeper into the mountainside for larger deposits.

Did Bronze Age people know anything, in fact, about mining at all? In Killarney there is evidence of mining going back 4,000 years; not for gold, but for copper, which they needed to make bronze. Several thousand years of settlement and fishing on the lakes during the Stone Age led to the discovery of copper ore deposits there.

There are still Bronze Age mines to show that the copper ore extraction took place. The technique used during the Bronze Age was to light wood-fuelled fires against the rock face that would weaken the mineralised rock, and the miners would have pounded it with stone hammers in order to extract it. The rock would have then been gathered in baskets

difficulty crushing the rock down. If you heat-treat it before quenching it, however, it makes the rock much more brittle, so it can be crushed up and the gold panned out. Only requir-

ABOVE Lakes of Killarney

and taken away to begin the smelting process. They were perhaps surprisingly sophisticated miners, so if there was gold to be had, there seems to be no doubt that they would have known exactly how extract it.

Next, heading to the Sperrin Mountains in Northern Ireland, where the task is to find out if the possibility of a Bronze Age gold mine could be a reality, and where it could have been in Ireland.

BELOW Gold lunula

The land we stand on now formed in a volcanic and turbulent time 600 million years ago. Gold comes from deep down in the earth's crust and moves along in fluid form. It rises towards the surface in cracks or faults in the earth's core. As it gets nearer the surface the temperature drops and where a fault has a bend in it, the fluid drops the minerals out, like a crystallisation process. The primary mineral that is formed is quartz that, as has been documented, carries gold with it. So, to find gold you follow the line of faults in the geological makeup of the area. The Sperrin Mountains are, however, covered in peat, so digging is required to investigate further.

A survey of the rocks has been carried out and the results plotted on a map. A fair amount of gold content was found concentrated in a number of places around the mountains. A mining company did in fact dig an exploratory shaft into the hillside 20 years ago to try and discover just how much gold there was, but it now lies abandoned.

It becomes clear just how difficult it would have been for the Bronze Age people to mine gold in the bedrock, because it so often occurs in such hard rock. If these rich veins ran to the surface, however, they wouldn't have had to mine.

With a silver percentage analysis of the Bronze Age gold artefacts complete, it in fact looks like the gold found at Croagh Patrick could be the

source of more Bronze Age gold than anywhere else. Although the landscape would have been very different at the time, without the covering of peat that is present today, rich gold seams rising to the surface would have been much more prevalent and is most likely the key to this mystery.

LEFT Bronze Age bracelet

Chapter 16

Figures in the Chalk

On the treeless chalk hills in the south of England there is a unique phenomenon not found anywhere else in the world – figures cut in the turf. There are about 30 of them altogether and the origins of some are quite mysterious, particularly the Long Man of Wilmington in Sussex. Who cut them? And for what reason? There must be a fascinating history behind these figures, and the evolution of this very distinctive chalk landscape.

One of the best-known hill figures is the White Horse at Uffington in Oxfordshire. Using a pioneering new technique, it is only recently that archaeologists have been able to date

the horse, and they believe it to be prehistoric; at least 500 years older than previously thought. Close up it is hard to decipher the horse shape and it looks like an abstract pattern, but from further away it can clearly be seen. It seems that it has survived because the local people have looked after it for nearly 3,000 years. The horse would in fact disappear under grass within a decade if it wasn't cared for.

In the 21st century the National Trust look after the maintenance of the horse, but the cleaning must have been done regularly for thousands of years. In order to put a date on the horse the archaeological team exca-

vated below the chalk. About four or five feet down they found the early silts from which they could analyse for dating purposes. The date they came up with – around 800 B.C. The White Horse of Uffington is in fact the only chalk figure that experts have accurately dated back that far.

The prehistoric date for the Uffington White Horse suggests that

ABOVE Cleaning of the Uffington White Horse

it was probably created by the same people who made other local ancient structures including a hill fort a couple of hundred of metres away. Does this suggest a Bronze Age trend for chalk carvings?

In Sussex, 120 miles away, lies another enigmatic chalk figure – the Long Man of Wilmington. Some think that this was also constructed in pre-historic times although no one really knows for sure. A team of archaeologists want to settle this mystery once and for all as many different dates have been suggested in the past. Some date it as Neolithic, and some Roman, but the most plausible argument according to the experts is an Anglo Saxon date. The reason: an ornamental belt buckle of the period has an

extremely similar figure carved on it, and this dates back to the 7th century. If they could date it accurately, it would then hopefully cast some light onto who made it in the first place and why. The silt collected at the foot of the Long Man should be dateable in the same way as the mystery of the Uffington White Horse was solved.

Why would this particular landscape have attracted prehistoric people? It was probably not for agriculture, as the chalk hills do not produce rich and fertile land. Chalk itself is very soft but contains a number of other materials within it, one of which was vital for prehistoric people – flint. There are in fact still traces of flint mines throughout the chalk landscapes of southern England where the prehistoric folk would have dug down to find great bands of horizontal flint seams. To get the best flint for their tools they would have had to dig about nine metres down using only naturally shed antler picks.

There is certainly a clear link between the chalk hills, the flint and prehistoric people. But that doesn't answer the question about why they carved what they did into the landscape.

The nearby hill fort at Uffington shows clear signs of a well-organised warrior community in which the horse would have played an important part in prehistoric society. The emergence of a kind of warrior aristocracy who mounted and learned to ride horses developed at this time. Horses were also highly important in terms of religion and symbolism and they were associated with death and resurrection. The Uffington White Horse is surrounded by the ancestral burial ground that was in use for nearly 3,000 years.

Another chalk figure, the Cerne Abbas Giant in Dorset is also of interest. Here also, arguments have raged over the history of the figure, which also has not been definitively dated.

LEFT Finglesham Man Buckle

in origin and was created to give honour to their Saxon god. Finally, there is a much later theory.

There are medieval ruins of Cerne Abbey that lie at the foot of the giant. During the 10th to the 16th centuries it was a very wealthy Benedictine abbey that owned all the land in the district, including the land on which the giant now stands. It seems inconceivable that these monks, who were dedicated to a life of prayer, abstinence and celibacy, would have tolerated a great big sexually exultant giant towering above them. They would also have had to regularly maintain it, otherwise it wouldn't be here today. Nowhere in the extensive surviving records from this time is there the slightest hint that the giant existed during this period in history. It therefore makes sense that the giant must have been created after the abbey dissolved in 1539.

In the Dorset archive in Dorchester, a document mentions the giant, and it appears in the churchwarden's accounts for the year 1694, itemised as 'for repairing the Giant'. Prior to that in 1617, there is a detailed survey of Cerne Abbas, and there is no mention whatsoever of the chalk carving. One

The earliest theory is that the Iron Age people, who lived in the area, cut him as part of their fertility celebrations. The second theory is that he is Roman, and the third that he is Saxon

theory is that a man called Denzel Holles, who was an MP and also owned Cerne Abbas, in fact created the giant. Hating everything Oliver Cromwell stood for, is it possible that Holles had the Giant created as a satirical figure?

Many of the other chalk figures in the area have records documenting their histories, yet horses undoubtedly dominate the theme. The horse at Westbury was cut in 1778, although

BELOW The Cerne Abbas Giant

FIGURES IN THE CHALK

BELOW Oliver Cromwell

the records suggest that this actually replaced a much older Anglo Saxon horse. The horse at Cherhill was cut in 1780, the horse at Alton Barnes in 1812, and the horse at Hackpen Hill was carved to mark Queen Victoria's coronation in 1837.

Although chalk carvings definitely started in prehistoric times, there seems to have been a particular craze for these figures in the 200 years after Cromwell. The southern England chalk hill landscape also lends itself particularly well to providing the perfect canvas for such carvings on which to make political or religious statements, or to mark important celebrations.

So, where does the Long Man fit into all of this in the end? The analysis of the soil sample and also pottery found at the bottom of the carving is given a mean age dating at around 1545 A.D. and not 1,000 years earlier as many people had thought, or hoped.

THE WESTBURY WHITE HORSE, WESTBURY HILL, BRATTON DOWN

ALSO AVAILABLE IN THE LITTLE BOOK SERIES

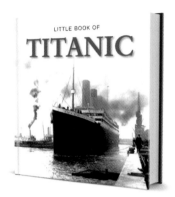

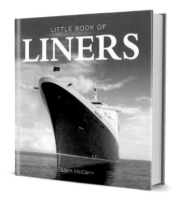

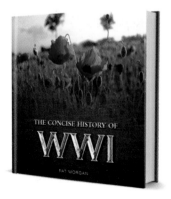

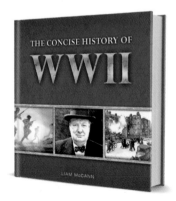

ALSO AVAILABLE IN THE LITTLE BOOK SERIES

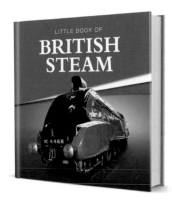

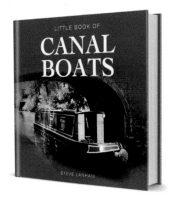

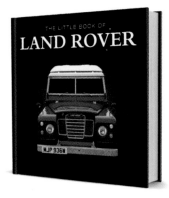

The pictures in this book were provided courtesy of the following:

WIKIMEDIA COMMONS

Design & Artwork: SCOTT GIARNESE & ALEX YOUNG

Published by: DEMAND MEDIA LIMITED & G2 ENTERTAINMENT LIMITED

Publishers: JASON FENWICK & JULES GAMMOND

Written by: MICHELLE BRACHET